There is not
fashion
to it

There is not fashion to it

selected poems

Thomas McAfee

edited by Ted Schaefer, Tricia Schaefer, Kay Callison,

Jerry Dethrow, and Greg Michalson

BkMk Press
University of Missouri-Kansas City

BkMk Press
University of Missouri-Kansas City
5101 Rockhill Road
Kansas City, Missouri 64110
(816) 235-2558 (voice)
(816) 235-2611 (fax)
bkmk@umkc.edu
www.umkc.edu/bkmk

Cover art: Thomas McAfee, collage of works
Author photo: Courtesy of Weatern Historical Manuscripts Collection
Robert Stewart (executive editor)
Ben Furnish (managing editor)
Susan L. Schurman (cover & book design)
BkMk Press wishes to thank Siara Berry, Megan Folken, & Blaire
Ginsburg. Thanks to Marcia Southwick for permission to reprint the
foreword by Larry Levis.

**Missouri
Arts Council**
The State of the Arts

Financial assistance for this project was provided by
the Missouri Arts Council, a state agency.

Library of Congress Cataloging-in-Publication Data

McAfee, Thomas, 1928-1982.
[Poems. Selections]
There is not fashion to it : selected poems / by Thomas McAfee ;
edited by Ted Schaefer, Tricia Schaefer, Kay Callison, Jerry Dethrow,
and Greg Michalson.
    pages ; cm
Summary: "Presents selected poems of Alabama-born Thomas
McAffee that remark on 20th Century American Life, specifically in
the Southern United States, recounts author's memories of family and
experiences through poetry, includes selections from author's writings-
in-dialogue with the Latin poet Catullus"-- Provided by publisher.
    I. Title.
    PS3563.A24A6 2015
    811'.54--dc23
                                        2014028810
ISBN 978-1-886157-96-5

in memory of Ted Schaefer

There is not **fashion** to it

From *Poems and Stories* (1960)

From *I'll Be Home Late Tonight* (1967)

From *The Body and the Body's Guest*
(1975)

From *Time Now* (1977)

From *The Tempo Changes. The Lights Go Up. The Partners Change.* (1978)

From *Flight* (1981)

From *My Confidant, Catullus* (1983)

I.

II.

Uncollected Poems

A Comma

Tom McAfee was our teacher, mentor, and friend. He died young, at 54, but his terse lyricism with its sardonic wit and singular voice lives on in our sensibilities, informing everything we write—and teach—even now. Early on, his students dubbed him "the master of omission." Indeed, from Tom we learned if nothing else to find the perfect word, to strive to strike the unnecessary from all we write or edit, to be left "holding necessity in . . . hand."

In spring 2010, the 30th anniversary of Tom's death in 1982 was just around the corner. Moved by these circumstances, and inspired by the newly appointed Poet Laureate Philip Levine, who wanted to revive the work of neglected authors, our friend and colleague Ted Schaefer, proposed assembling a selection of Tom's work. Enlisting his wife Tricia and the three of us as collaborators, Ted had us exchange our personal McAfee archives of books, literary magazines, copies of occasional poems, and correspondence by mail, along with our "picks" for inclusion in the manuscript. At some point, Tricia started the painstaking process of typing copies of our selections, eventually preparing a finished manuscript to be formatted for submission to publishers. We then gathered for a long weekend in September 2010 in Columbia, Mo., first to go through Tom's archive at Western Manuscripts Collection of the State Historical Society of Missouri, searching for work we might have missed, including published poems that had not been collected. Finally we sat down together to winnow what we had into a manuscript of manageable length, work that continued in the weeks to come, thanks to Ted's diligence and Tricia's patience and stamina at the keyboard.

Finally, a story: Tom was an avid correspondent, and one of the unexpected pleasures of this project was getting to share especially Ted Schaefer's voluminous cache of McAfee letters, dug out of boxes in his Lake Geneva, Wisconsin, attic. But Tom's favorite correspondence was with his father. From time to time he would share these letters with his friends, and point to how they always ended their letters not with a period, but a comma: More to come. So it is with the passing of any artist. There is no period at the end, but a comma followed by the body of their work, which becomes the ongoing property of their readers. We turn these poems, which continue to mean so much to us, over to you, concluding this volume not with a period, but a comma,

—The Editors

The Anatomy of Saturday Night

To the uninitiated or casual reader, Thomas McAfee's poems might seem calm, even reasonable. Certainly they establish themselves quietly in the mind, the way a familiar room does when the occupant returns to it and the light brings things softly to order. If the room in these poems weren't the room of a total stranger, a stranger even to the poet, such a return would be reassuring. It is not.

And if Thomas McAfee is unique among poets now at work, it is not because, merely, he risks unfreezing the available diction, the *available reality*, by using words such as *rosaceous, Leviticus,* and *topless bar* in the same short poem. That feat is, of course, unique enough if only because it defends poetry from the deadening, small-town tourism that so many poets adopt, unwittingly or nostalgically, when they take up the subject of a small town or rural life. But to describe Kansas in terms of clichés about Kansas is to stay in the bar of the Holiday Inn. McAfee *does* write about the small town; his power and his misfortune is that he writes from *inside* that town, that life; he never waves from the Interstate. There is a terrible way in which this poet and these poems are condemned to live in America, in what is left, now, of a rural and Midwestern America that seeks everywhere, in the sinew of these poems, its own demise and dismemberment.

Whether the poem is elegiac or satirical, the landscape is interior, private; it leads dismayingly inward to the place where the animal invented by sorrow dwells. McAfee's passage there, however dignified, is also a passage like that of a king's through the guts of a beggar; it is a torture. That is why the barmaids with roses behind their ears in these poems *located* in Kansas, or Missouri, or Alabama, are insane. His poems invite comparison to those of Weldon Kees because McAfee's knowledge of terror is as complete as Kees'. But the long poem "Translating in Brazil" is a catalogue of such terrors by an original poet who survives even his own hells through increasingly sophisticated maneuvers and through a style so hard and unsentimental that the reader, upon suddenly seeing himself in such poems, in such mirrors, blinks.

—Larry Levis
Columbia, Missouri, 1978

from

Poems and Stories
(1960)

The Matriarch

You in your bounty—your hair scented gray—
Walked tall among the petunias and your boys.
Slender, Bible-quoting, you had your say
On wars and marriage vows and proper toys
For grandchildren.

          When your family-prayed on Sunday nights—
The living room a crowd of things to do—
Each prudely solemn word defined your rights.
Tense wives cursed the scent of lavender, and the blue
You wore. But you ignored any narrowed eye
Which sparkled out against the truths you made.

Good woman: boys get bored, petunias seed, we die.
You did, holding tight to things that fade.
At your grave, veiled wives stood upright, wanting to know
Why their glad husbands wept to see you go.

The Saga

Aunt Alice big as a barrel,
Always an old-dress smell—
Sweat and rose cologne—

Was Gallic when she met me,
With smothering hugs and kisses,
Too wet and adoring.

I'd run away from her.
"Where is the child, where?"
As I shook behind the juniper.

But sometimes she was fun:
A casket lid undone,
She cried and screamed like sixty.

For funerals were her game:
Petals nearly drooping
Before her happy rage.

Now my sons hide from her
(Her generation's dead),
Hide behind my legs.

And I must lift them up—
Almost in sacrifice—
To smother in her bosom.

A Dream of the South

Although divine disunity
Reigns there—the broganed
One-eyed man explains
Courtly gestures to a child,
A sunken garden shelters
Rusty fenders—although
Time itself has ruptured,
The feelers of my brain
Reach back to the sun.

It is unpleasant spring
Here in this other country.
Just a few of the trees
Have budded, only
Crocuses have bloomed.
There's been cold rain
Each day for a week.
                    But a month ago, a letter
Told me:
                    The jonquils
Are all in bloom.
Tom, you should see
The tulips. They're. . .

I see cold rain
Through a window
That goes darker;
I know that this ordered

World is corrupt,
It will not grow,
The sun won't corrupt it.

I think of pine trees,
I think of margins of flowers,
I long for a horse grazing,
I reach back to the sun.

The Photograph of My Grandparents

To hide the sooted fireplace stood their youth,
A photograph within an ornate frame.
Whatever meaning pictures have, what truth
To last beyond a life, was here to blame.

Posed beside her, taller, and serene,
He was defiance for the hardest year;
And she, dressed in a gown that once was clean,
Looked fiercely straight into the far and near.

When I saw the picture last, her gown
Was speckled with the ash of many fires;
And dust and web-cracks made a smiling clown
Of that serenity which time admires.

Search out the farthest rooms and you will find
Not anywhere the action and the guilt.
The photograph is stored away, and kind
To them. This is the falling house they built.

Fragment About Poetry

Out of his own irrelevance he wove
Down the chaotic snow-fallen street.
It was irregular there for snow at all,
And his feet were not made for the slickness.
He fell several times, belching.
                            Ripped coat,
Bad nerves—he took it all in stride.

He cursed eloquently mother, God, and wife.
He put it all together, some snow-brilliant way,
Clichés and all—divined bad breath, general stutter,
Cough—and caught it all suddenly
In amaranth and rhythm, and walked home
Straighter than he could.

The Last Peacock's Last Feather

I
The last peacock has lost this feather.
It is, besides dark amber, a reminder
Of the underlayers of serpentine.

On earth there are so many peacocks,
And every feather holding half of what
The senses are. And more: below,

The streams of cochineal, the fishless
Eyes of green, the greedy
Turquoise mouths that never tasted food.

II
Besides in form, there is a textbook
In the aesthetics of all that ever was,
And all that never shall be seen. . .
In this diamond's reflection.

If this were the last peacock's last feather,
It would last longer than the mouth
Of any moth, and would shine brighter
Than the eye of any human mind.

The Unhappy Few

—After reading Weldon Kees

Most of us spend most of our lives
Climbing in and out of wombs,
Bitching about bad coffee and too wet
Martinis. Most of us lust for, more than love,
Our wives, waitresses, and celluloid sirens.

But a few seem to move to the total horror
Of ennui, to wake tired at morning,
To be glad to face another alley, rather
Than go on for another hour with the sheets,
Fighting the nightmares that gang up.

Those few are real and positive. They know
What misery and terror really are.
They're usually the very last ones to bitch.
They go off somewhere to drink in a bar
Or cry or quietly to kill themselves.

Bats in the Philippines

She told me that in the Philippines,
As they all sat on the veranda,
Bats would come up in hordes—
Small-bodied bats with great wingspread—
Like clouds of rain.

While they all sat, she said,
With their bamboo glasses
And smelled the beginnings of evening,
They remarked the bats only an instant
Between the casual gossip.

Now, she said, those miles away
And years away, she remembered the bats
But none of the talk,
Not one living soul!
Except a young man, exceedingly drunk,
Who told her bats were important.

The Border

My mother's border grew on a clean dirt mound;
No weeds undid its pure formality.
Some years dark-blood verbena laced and wound
Among itself, but never wild, never free.
Whatever flower stood on guard, it found
A raging land of colors there, a sea
Of grass the other way. Boys turned around,
They might expect some instant laxity
On the border's part: purple asters now unbound,
With rose petals shattering mutinously.
And boys might never know a woman's hands
Work always early mornings, pulling weeds.
The woman, with wet shears, who understands
What ruthless care the clean and formal needs.

At Table . . .

At table, feet must be flat on the floor.
Don't cross your legs. If something spilled, ignore
It. Spread your napkin out, first thing, across
Your lap. Eat some of all. It's *your* loss
If you don't. Why once I couldn't eat
An oyster raw, and now—what a treat!
Don't fidget when your uncle says a long blessing;
He means it all. Besides, he's always stressing
You to God. You should be glad you've got
So many relatives who care a lot
About you. When you've finished eating and
Must go, excuse yourself before you stand.
This is how a gentleman should act.
It's manners now but later will be tact.

So spoke my Mother, many and many a time,
These words, adultly, only not with rhyme,
And guiltily I sit today, to eat
Not minding my napkin right or my truant feet,
But nevertheless I *know*, as I used to know
What was sin and, where the comma should go.

In Time of Sickness

Two years ago, counting back from January. . .
In Alabama a kind of wintry, wary
Spring had begun. Next month camellias would open,
In March the jonquils, then anything could happen
As far as flowers were concerned. You yearned
For them that spring, I know it, Mother,
Lying on patched hospital sheets, smothering
(Cold, cooped up) in a dinky room, its walls
Tranquility-gray. You lay there, a hand-knitted shawl,
The color of honey, around your shoulders;
It was wintry in Alabama, ever colder
As camellias budded and suddenly burst.
Though icy, this was the warmest of the worst
Three winters you know. Your flowers were worked by the man
(He talked to himself; so what?) you used to stand
Over at seventy-five cents an hour. Many years,
Many words taught him the art of hoe and shears.

Easter, I wasn't aware of the "ritual story"—
Nothing new to wear, broke, playing with the glory
Of being mortal. Tons of Greyhound bus
Moaned through the wind, coldly delivering us
To wedding beds, fresh wars, new griefs.
I studied the faces around me, sleeping and brief.
I read in a smutty newspaper that emotion

Could now be applied like a facial lotion.
New Year! cut the adder's head in two!
I'm poisoned with fear. I'm poisoned with love too.

Summer scolds
The yard today; verbena droops; blind moles
Cave through the earth, leaving line-mounds of lawn.
I, incompetent as ever, am drawn
Back to your winter days. Rich fawning ferns
Remind me they need water. The sky burns.

from

I'll Be Home Late Tonight
(1967)

Extreme Unction: Act Three

I think you've gone the limit,
love, throwing glasses,
shooting off
at the mouth,
parading yourself
and myself, too,
to the wide wide world.
—Do your jungle duties
at home, where the flushing's loud
and no one can hear you yell.
—And keep all your minor
jealousy
in the cage of your own
sullen self.
—First thing, and last,
don't call me up
at some swank hour,
like noon,
to apologize.

Woman of Another Time

Ladies, she said, and gentlemen never chew gum.
Ladies never whistle, she said, nor do gentlemen hum.
I think of this these million miles away
In time. I check the Birmingham Airport sky. What would she say
About the jet Electra there
Rubbing its nose to the wind? Or care?
She who would not go up—nor near water—and not into
    Mammoth Cave!
Still, she checked off the ones who would, and gave
Each one his check, against or for
His valor, but not in terms of water or wings or caves or even war.
Rather, in terms of chewing gum, of saying *thank you please,*
Of whistling—these
Were her tests of whether man defied the dust or not.
Indecorous, he might fly to the moon and come back, and still rot.

Certain as the Mare My Father Gave Me

Certain as the mare my father gave me,
Certain as the country, winding ride
Across the afternoon, was that small time
Of quiet which I knew each night before
My father said goodnight and turned from me.

I remember one green afternoon
Of summer when I rode my mare. We crossed
The Old Pike's Bridge, and down below I saw
A car-top. Only that above the water.
I rode away from it into the hills.

After I had put the mare away,
Had eaten supper and undressed for bed,
My father came to me and then I told
About the car. And he made certainty
That hour, and let me sleep with his goodnight.

Imaginary Voyages

Imaginary voyages, over the blue brilliance
of glossy paper, do not interest me.
The gray-haired lady at the travel agency
may keep her splashy folders of romance.
I have no longing for camels, Hilton hotels
in unpronounceable countries, sherbets in the desert.
There are always lice and bed bugs. Probably the wells
are dry. Some hard ancient hurt in a peasant's eye
will be too much of right here
to make me sweat in my mind
to trek over there.

Henry Gentle

Henry Gentle, bloated with too much butter
And sugar on biscuits at breakfast and supper,
Talked about the Bible the way you'd talk
About it if you wrote it.
He'd lean on the mantel or sit
On his cane-bottom chair
And carouse with the angels and devils and afternoon air
In his antique, hightower parlor.
Nothing belied his purity but his color,
Which was red, red
As a young cock's comb.
He spoke of disaster gingerly. At home
He was against picture shows.
Downtown, he was against Hitler and loved Roosevelt.
All the time though, bless his heart, he had a wide old belt
That diminished and diminished.
When I see his impromptu grave now where he's finished
His obese talking
I know angels want to be garrulous and temporal and sing.

In These Caves

What do bones do
In these caves?
Rains come hard,
With winds,
And fill the bottoms.
What do bones do?

They navigate the bottoms
And the tops.
They enliven the darkness.
They talk to bats.
They are white.
With lightning. They linger.

When you see me next
Among some Cherokees,
Be dear,
Touching the mold.
Think of eyelids,
Think of hair.

In the Red

Q: Why do elephants drink?
A: To forget.

I see the herd of them—their ragged skin
Warming against the formal afternoon sky—
As they sit, like lumps, for cocktails to begin.
"I think back on each conjugal lie

I've told," they wheeze; and this is their party talk.
Their skin goes red from gray as the sun descends.
"Wouldn't it be tranquility-grand to walk
Innocent at dawn, fresh and at loose ends?"

They drink themselves ad nauseam till three,
When a cynical moon throws a little light, to lunge home.
Guilty insomniacs in their misery
They squint, all trembling, into the jungle, alone.

The Hereford Bull at Dawn

The Hereford bull—
His underside low to the ground—
Munches till his belly is full,
And makes little sound.

And he will not eat too much.
He minds his girth.
Vanity, as such,
Arrived at birth.

A pasture backs him up.
Beyond the pasture, trees.
And more beyond, a sun comes up
As if to please

The Hereford bull.
There's elegance in his stance
As he eats till his belly is full,
With never a side glance.

Aristocratic ton,
Garlanded with pride,
He moves away from everyone
With everyone at his side.

For Mary Lou Williams,
at Piano, at the Hickory House

Not one for schmaltz, not for moxie;
And I cannot improve her
In poetry: her fingers black
And growing to the ivory keys
And to the black: her wide eyes
Closed.

—My heart and head reach out.
I think of a dark Madonna without child.
Behind her, two dark wise men, bass and drummer,
Beat out their adoration.

That's My Boy

My God if I ever hear
another father
at another liquor luncheon
(whiskey sour and/or martini)
in a dinky hotel
announce how his son did
in High football. . .
—I mean, how he did
that night
when Scooter was playing too.
Who's Scooter the hell?
He's something for fathers
and mothers
to live on—
the way they live on
their ineffectual boy
whose future ended
two years ago
and who will soon be
in the employ
of I.B.M.
—His hair, oh Lord, is
miraculously parted.

On the Porch at the Rest Home

They plant me here on this screwball porch.
The door is locked and I can't shave. But the moon
comes up. I stare at it as long as I can.
The sun hurts my eyes. Who can rock to Bethlehem?
—They all go away. I want to go.
I take my head in my hands like this
and I ram my head and I ram my head
till all the flies fly away.
Oh, the people come back. I know they will.
They put a lizard in my head. It scrambles around
for a little while, till they go away, then I go away.
We do it every day.

My Lady of the Black Raincoat

I.
I light a cigarette and see by the flame
it's two o'clock. Where are you tonight?
Whose blood are you sucking? Who do you mount?
 —Last night when it rained
you came to my window,
and I let you in.
                    Naked
beneath the black raincoat
you lay beside me and fed
me sleeping pills. And then
you left. Where did you go?
This morning they pumped my stomach.
Why did you leave me?

II.
Sometime come to me
when the sky is June
and birds are blue
and red on the grass,
when there is an oak
tree moving with wind.
Then let me see your face,
my love. For once, out
of shadows. For once, by day.
This is a dare.

III.
You are My Lady of the Soot,
of the Spider's Belly, of the
Wild Pig's Squeal.

        My wrist
against the razor blade
tells me you're as real as
nausea and delirium and
electric shock racing the bones.
You're My Lady of the Stones,
My Lady of Dry Spittle,
of the Black Raincoat,
of Despair.

from

The Body and the Body's Guest

(1975)

Being Dull

I have tried to strip
the unnecessary:
the showy clothes, the food
neither good nor needed,
the metaphors that are
themselves, the killing
adjectives, small talk,
big talk. And so, I'm dull,
holding necessity in my hand.

Larry Levis Has a Poem
About Writing a Poem

You had all the advantages.
First of all, you wanted
to write a poem. You had
somewhere to go and something
to slick your hair back
about. I sat in that damned
airport and wasn't going
anywhere. I was leaving,
and I had a long time to wait.

Opening Scene

The maid enters:
Has the master arisen?
The butler, arranging his jacket:
No. This is Sunday. Then the corpse
is still in the closet.
—The corpse is still
in the closet? And the master doesn't know?
—Yes. The corpse is nicely
wrapped in newspapers. Nothing
to think about till Monday.
Shall we sport us in another closet?
The maid, demurely:
If you are sincere. And don't think
it crude. Oh pity the corpse!
—We could join him, poor fellow.
—I think that's dear. Let's sport us.

A Note to the Beloved

Should you not want to wear
the yellow dress, I shouldn't
expect you? Is this what
I'm to understand? And I'm
To wait, whatever, in the
lobby, expecting you in
the yellow dress or not at
all? I simply don't understand.
Could you explain what the
yellow dress has to do with
your not appearing in the lobby?
Am I to spend the day wondering
about the blue dress and
the green dress?

The Visitor

Too bad you came when you did.
Nothing but rain and cold.
Wrong season, you kept
repeating, as you waited
by the window. You would stare
at the row of cacti on the ledge.
The chair took your shape.

Now look at the hills—
if you could. They are green.
Sun and shadows bounce together,
play on the chair you made.
No one in all this house, not even
the bachelor uncle, remembers your face.

Wife to Husband

You tell me I must change
my life. I know, and I do
constantly, and not because
of you. You: you my darling
are a rat's nest of seven years.
There is nothing much more to say.
In bed, you're weird.
"You must change your life!"
I know where you got the quote.

Suicide: Day Thoughts on Death

Standing on that window ledge
over there—if I dared, for I'm
afraid of heights—I'd take a look
at all the people, take a look
at the later furor, especially in newspapers,
and remember: *Your name should
appear in the paper only three times:
when you're born, when you're married,
and when you die.*

              Possibly, just
possibly, I might give some thought
to suicide, if I could be on an island
way off Tahiti and if there were no newspapers
and if suicide were common or unheard of.

Pearl Harbor Day, 1974

In the Three Cheers Lounge, I order
my orange juice—it's been
a long time since a drink—and Rose
hands it to me and says, *This is*

Pearl Harbor Day. I recall, of course,
that Sunday, when the radio gave the news,
and I rushed to the front porch, to
deliver it. I was too young to drink

from the glamorous tall glasses of my elders.
Today—after Korea, Vietnam, so many
wars we can't remember—I, arthritic,
taking some kind of blessed medicine,

am again forbidden what Three Cheers everywhere
provide. Again, I'm where I started.
On the backward landscape, I see bright bones
and pain and pain that bore pain.

It would be logical to order a gin on
the rocks and another and spend the afternoon
watching Christmas shoppers or TV football
or just getting drunk.

Stories of an Evening

The front-porch stories of a summer
evening—the lightning bugs are crushed
jewels on the children's arms—
teach us more of the heredity
of sparrows
and the future declensions of our
stranger cousins
than all the treeless
and starless makeshift
of logic. Grossness of touch
has left us below the
murky surface
where fish begin to walk.

For instance: the story of
second cousin Ruth, who
slipped off to Birmingham, and
took her a hotel room
at the top, and laid out
her jewels on the white bedspread,
and jumped.
            Lord, the stars
in their hot inhuman magnificence
are startled by that, and
the lightning bugs—their

phosphorous the last
to breathe—take second
breath at the telling.

Not even the FBI
could tell you why this is,
it is so deeply involved
with breathing: even the stream
through the violet's
stem.

The fish, as they
beat through the thickening
mud, knew something, and
they drank dark air. The stars,
aware of something, shuddered
at those growing legs.

Suicides of Poets

a wyld infirmyte. . .

—James Hoccleve

1.

It was the other day in the Park
At the turn of the Pike
That he hanged himself.
I didn't know his name.
It was two o'clock or so
In the morning when
The papers found the body
Headed by nineteen years
Of skin and muscle pulling down.
Caught by the eye of the paperboy,
Who caught him, abstracter than fog
(The paperboy abstracted from
His rolls of orange comics),
He was caught by nothing but wet ground.

2.

Some bear up,
Some are poisonous,
Some are edible, some are
Beautiful splotches of opal
And confusion.
They are that.
Some are tree trunks.

They are that.
No matter how green ferns are
Or how wet morning grass is
Or how slippery spring soil is
Or how reassuringly tough or brittle
Dead bark is
Some bear up.
Poison and love swear at each other
Like mean morning birds.

3.

27 June, 1966
The top of my head has gone up
Like a balloon held
By a bad child and
On a diminishing string.
The child has pulled it back
Like a miracle, pricked it
With a devil's pin.

4.

I think I killed myself.
I think my voice
Has the sound of a golf ball
Just driven. Come back to me

Angels struck in bad marble
Here to these satin tombs
Where my heart has gone worse and worse.

There is a mammoth wrecking crane
Filling the air with milk.
I haven't seen for a year except
The pearl of these walls.
I slept too long last night.
I woke from a nightmare
Wondering at teeth and fingernails and hair.

5.
The gossip here
Is ruthlessly ordinary.
I can hear.
I've not heard
For eighteen weeks.

One day put me together
And fly me down the lawn
Like a kite. That wouldn't be
Resurrection.
Let out the string to the North Pole.

6.

I walk through earth.
I stumble over the roots
Of my hanging-tree.
(I must settle the paperboy's mind.)
It is like the sea
When seaweeds tie your ankles together.
It is earth and sea gone together.
They want your fingernails,
Blue or fish-bone white,
To claw or fish.
Oh, they beckon beckon,
Will rescue you only in stasis,
An island refusing to be flooded
Since time.
They call by muddy waves.

7.

Water and oil,
The body has gone from the heart,
The knees reverberate.
The trees die in the morning,
The sparrows were late
And lucky. Tell the wind
We are not at midnight even.

Feet are the finer part
Of living. Toes nudge and sing.
Hair on the head
Is a fine beginning.
Let me be at eleven o'clock.

8.
My darling, who you are,
Please stop me.
My bones have left each other,
Are ploughing their separate ways.
I sulk, I weep, do Zion
Through the universe. . .
I'd settle and nurse on the lava.
I tried, my love.
Angels chipped from bad stone
Are better.

The Body and the Body's Guest

—to the memory of Dan Schroeder

I.

A week five days in the grave, where are you? Time
Is not real this time, except in parts, those parts
That have to do with the necessary days: tolerable crime
In the headlines, sleeping with pills, practicing all the arts
Of putting Time away, waking to nightmares, saying,
"I can erase the time and the action and the place, by praying."
Simply praying. The *News* reminds me this is the dog days.
My mind is tousled. Where do your atoms go? It rains,
Is Sunday, as if it knew these are the ways
We speak of grief. At last, what does Time do to the brain's
Potential? No answer. The *News* says this is the dog days.
Then Christmas, Easter . . . The *News* says this is the dog days.

II.

Does anything move there, or sound, in that cemetery
I haven't seen? Here, in another climate, now, all the sound
Is a gentle rain, on the roof and on the pond, and frogs
Off there at the far bank of the pond. Your heart is stopped,
Could it be there is silence exact, with no one to stroll
By the graves, and hear his own heart toll? I would pay
Someone to stroll always; for rain; for insect sounds.
I would pay resurrected saints to toll the bell, walk the grounds.

III.

Morning. The sun, somehow, is out again,
Festooning, you'd like to think, and the vague, dedicated man
Across the street power-mows his lawn. You don't hear.
Here is a wide room of parochial waking up. Fear
And trembling were last night, today are words,
With the cigarettes and coffee and the waking, and birds
Outside amazed at the grass. All is not well,
You learn, as the sleep wears off, and the dead one starts to tell
What it's like, and you think you know, already, too well.

IV. ANOTHER MORNING

Can the first light be killing, dawn, awakener, when
Closed blossoms open and furled fronds unfurl
And the mist lifts from the pond and the horses and
Cattle go about their business and the man still struck
With sleep attunes himself to the sun? Perhaps you look
At the sky and long for the troubled sleep, even
The nightmares that left you sweating. For this is truly
A Death Parade, each thing, from spider to rose,
A testament of death. The first light is a signal
To the last. First light, the voices from the grave are deafening.

V.

The sun is merciless, the air is worse after rain, those
Flowers are blooming that seem to thrive on disaster:
Marigolds, zinnias, petunias. Summer, mindless, goes
Doggedly towards something—we, waiting and grieving, prefer
Towards something, if we must wait and grieve by those
Flowers we would not pull, and would not take to the grave.
At noon the dead, attacked by the sun, seem to close
Their mouths and sleep, for they, though brave
And living the final disaster, consumed, chose
Nothing, or little, and live confused in space
And among tree roots. Walking earth's green, perhaps they chose
This final disaster, which goes on, and will erase
Their eyes and feet. No matter, now, at noon, what they chose.

VI.

Finally, and finally, and finally, we come to this:
The dead one lies in the grave, the motion we knew
Is gone, the enduring face is gone, the brain
Is rotted away, the odor of the corpse would leave
Us blind and sick. All our philosophies, Einsteinian
Leaps, our faith and hope do not recall the voice,
As it was, that we knew. The laughter is lost.

There Is Not Fashion to It

There is not fashion to it. Seasons extend it. Time
pays it tribute, however clumsily. Death, at its door, is wary
and walks away. Death is not yet conditioned
to its style. One thing: whatever its name, the name
itself will change like fashion: your fault, and yours,
and mine and mine. No matter.

1.
In the act of my deed, I lie like the moon.
Like Hal, now Henry, wooing Kate and saying the words don't
matter, I lie in the act of saying. Shakespeare's Kate,
aware of the lie, was pleased. Henry, still Hal,
was Falstaff in his wooing. Kate could have wept,
had she not been so pleased.

2.
It's the place in the mighty diamond the jeweler
has to find before he wields. It all could go wrong.
I must speak to you circuitously. I must
Give an example and ask, Why does Clodia, bitch-woman,
sit so high in your mind? And everything
petty in Rome that Catullus left you? No one
has got that sparrow right since he left. Even your
great-great grandfather was aware of it, and he
sweetened things and messed them up the best he could.

3.

One learns not to say too much. One becomes afraid
to speak at all.

Is it the night of the soul
imperative?

Why could Einstein never rest?
Why do the atoms of Leonardo beat against
the windows?

There's something else outside.
I see the sheep. I see the scene I saw last night and
can't put down. I told the sheep goodbye
for that time only. I left them with a world
of questions to answer. (Hegel said
philosophy is worthless.) Though my friends
are worthless at answering questions, they
respond immensely to Catullus and the words
of Shakespeare's Cleopatra when she died.

4.

More out of ignorance, I think, than desperation
we say *eternity*. Then: rivets into the sides
of eternity, eternity being mist in the valley.

I mustn't say what to say, for fear
of you, that you will dismiss me.

5.

It may be ignorance, it may not make the curves
of infinity, it may topple like an old house
that has had dignity and been in your family long,
it may never be known by your wife (even when
you are one and are known by her), it does not dry
with the rain, it is not fashion, seasons extend it.

from

Time Now
(1977)

Teaching the South

(At the beginning of the course, the teacher conducts a tour of the South. First lesson begins in North Alabama. The teacher speaks.)

Although those peacocks by the pond have nothing
To do, directly, with what we're talking about,
Don't let them out of your sight. This is Winston
County, called Free State of Winston. Because
It got, so to speak, its dander up
At all the seceding and what it thought
Was vain-glory. Practicality—
You had to be practical here—was part
Of it. That peacock lost his tail last summer.
As you can see, spring has begun this early
In January. Notice how the new
Feathers are richer in off-shades—those
Brassy-green-blues—and how they look more
Delicate—*tenderer* is the word I want,
But it's not right—than the other
Feathers. Cousins fought their cousins. Later,
In a book, you'll see how the counties around
Moved like wolves into here. It was not
Just food they wanted. They wanted something dear
And secret, and they knew where it was. Food—
It did not matter, except for the very old
And the children, to these people in Winston.
Free State of Winston: I like the sound of it.

In the midst of that War, in the midst
Of its neighbors and kin, it mustered
Five companies of infantry soldiers
For the Union. No, the neighbors and
Cousins didn't know what to do, at *first*
And so they took, like children, all the food,
The clothes, the relics handed down. They should
Have known, even at first, it had to be
Something dearer. Then when one day they knew,
They knew right where to find it. The peacocks
Are following *him*, the one with the new feathers,
To the woods. It's hard to feature peacocks
In the woods. You think of them with men
Dressed up for Sunday and ladies in finery.
They say they ploughed each other—having no
Recourse. They say they ate acorns and bark,
And greens, poke salad, cooked without grease
Or salt. So they lived, at first on spirit sap
And stubborn leather limbs and . . . Then
Their cousins and neighbors began to come,
To take their sons away, then them, the fathers,
To work as slaves in the bounding counties.
Some people still won't speak. If you look
Very close, to the left, you'll see that peacock
In that low oak beside the four pine trees.

He wants to be the leader now that his
Feathers are back and brilliant. He'll never
Learn that the varmints in the woods care just
Enough to eat those feathers up.

Four in the Morning

The sky is choosing its color. Above the pine tops
Violet moves into gray. Off, thunder
Makes the distance. Del, the quarter horse,
Is white down the hill, mixed with mist.
Objects that hold me prisoner are prisoner
Of the light. Deep above me, lightning
Cracks at nothing. I know I'm here.
It is August.

        Up the road, at Bethel Church,
It is August forever. The graves sing out in silence.
As you would have it, they need no comfort.

Gardens

When my mother died
My father grew
His own particular kind
Of garden: vegetables.

Weeds protected
Those sick-white tomatoes
No bigger than
A little girl's fist.

And scrawny corn
Not half-made,
And the okra grown
Too long and hard.

My mother never cared
For vegetable gardens.
There were nice cool markets
And a boy to help you.

My father always said
That if you grew them
Yourself, they were better.
But his failed because

The hired man failed to take
Interest in vegetables.
He liked beef, just beef,
Served at a café in town.

Conversion

There is a dentist office there,
Brighter than any rouge
My grandmother ever wore.
It is whore-rouge brick.

The trick of the affair:
Her house,
Inelegantly Victorian,
Snow-weathered gray throughout
The Alabama sun,
A disheveled soul reared
Too high from its foundation—
Her monster full of collapse
Might never have cursed it out
Where all is serene now,
A deadly green of lawn
Without a bump.

To a mother pulling her first-born
From a Pontiac,
There was nothing here before
What's here right now.

And the dentist is kind.
Young, he still wears

College clothes. His nurse
Is his wife, his wife

Is his nurse: a girl so remote
From a bloody tooth
There is no blood.

All is serene,
Except I see
An old woman,
Raised out of hell,
Her rags on fire,
Crossing the perfect lawn,
Crossing the almost-perfect lawn.

Time Now

Nothing, nobody — but God and maybe
The illusion of memory—can gather together
The horses, sheep, the peacocks and the cattle,
The wise ducks
He thinks of as what he was.
                              So he,
The weathered child-man, mumbles his way
Out of the century. He prepares to greet
Old men, their ghosts in overalls,
Ambling down the city streets and leading
mules.
But the men (he thinks they were young
In a dream he had) look down at their
Colorless shoes, and the mules, out of
Eyes distant and unspeaking as dead
Ponds, almost reflect something.

But don't. He is not who, what, where
He was. For all he knows, he never
Existed. Sometimes on dark afternoons
He sits by a stingy table lamp
And reads about himself in a novel.

from

The Tempo Changes.
The Lights Go Up.
The Partners Change.

(1978)

The Music

1.

Handmade in Austria, the Bösendorfer piano
Is Imperial Grand beneath a plastic drop-sheet.
Only a hundred are made each year.
He poisoned to hear the music he imagined.
In turn—as invisible finger pressed
The elephant tusks—he was murdered.
His bashed brain thought it heard the violent Bach.

2.

What is a *darkening face?* What is a face
That darkens when it reads the letter written
On cream-colored paper or answers the phone
When the cocktail party is two-thirds over?
How dark does it get? The color of night
Without a moon? Does it darken all at once
Or shade to shade or very gradually?

3.

The Baccarat crystal dangled from the chandelier.
Once a week, a servant washed and polished
Each drop of it. No one ever sat on the gilded

Chairs to hear the clutter of Vivaldi. So no one
Was threatened by a falling chandelier or music
Going mad as it does in movies. One face darkened,
Though. Dig up the grave and open the coffin and look.
The eyes and ears are ladened with a darkened face.

4.
The *fog-draped morning*, the *chenille coverlet*,
The undertaking parlor with colonial façade, the
Prep room where the body is embalmed—these are
Clues in a murder mystery, leading to what
He thought was music and where it should be played.

Eclipse: Los Angeles Adventure

Houdini and palm trees are promissory notes
All the evenings I take my walks: my feet and brain
Unleashed, my heart prepared as a Boy Scout,
My arthritic hands ready to swim.

I could send my wife searching for jungle adventure.
She might return with baskets of rosaceous fruit;
She might be gobbled up; she might amble in
At midnight, talking about movie stars and
Crocheting and what her mother said about Leviticus.

Too much chance involved. Chance and luck abide.
I might miss myself coming out of a topless bar,
A bottomless pit on Vine, the sun's corona,
The nip and tuck of an almost-perfect human.

Luck is chancy, and so forth. I might never be
Myself, might die in the chromosphere, too near and red
To know. This is a wonderful neon night.
I am alone with gaudy boys and girls, palm trees,
Summer/winter, what I'll be, yelling music, the heavens.

At Home, Far Away Inside

First, let us move away,
                    but leave behind us
The grand piano, the Steuben glass, books and
Phonograph records, what might distract us,
And since this is a real journey—surrounded
By stars and their shadows and what is beyond
Them—we will not travel.

We sit all day and night and watch the moths
Eat our clothes. Each tiny separate eye of the compound
Eye searches for the cashmere overcoat, and finds it,
Eats it as we gasp.
                    The Oriental rugs are eaten,
The upholstery of our chairs, the corks
In the bottles of wine.

Deep in the journey, the clothes we wear become
Antiques. Then we, keen of eye as the moth,
See our genitals, our navels
Which we have never praised before.
We are naked, new, overcome, and prepared.

It is the marvelous journey,
We are near death.

We say, *Look! Look!*
These are discoveries we
May not see again:
Seven hundred wonders and more, obliterations, birth
Happening all at once.
We are breathless as children.

Uncle Ezra on Rainy Days

Uncle Ezra has skipped again:
The bedspread is gone, all
The windows in his room are open,
And, most important, the goldfish
In the pond are missing. He has
Gone somewhere to free them.

He always leaves on rainy days.
I think to let the rain come in.

He should be in New York
By now, checking in at the
Chelsea. A bedspread, a bucket
Of goldfish, and a small valise
With his diary and some clothes.

"A week, at the most," he tells
The desk clerk. "Yes, Uncle Ezra,
And about the goldfish?" "I'll
Find a big aquarium. That's not
Freedom — but suggest something else."

He never stays much longer
Than a day and night. The bedspread
Over the Chelsea bed, the windows

Open, *Do Not Disturb* on the door,
The goldfish free, the diary blank—
And Uncle Ezra takes a jet back here.
We welcome him back in the sunshine.

Brothers Meeting

"Voici le soir charmant, ami du criminel..."
—Baudelaire

The two of you stay where
You are. The streetlight
Won't stretch to here.
The police won't walk in
These shadows. You are brothers.
It's time you met.

Don't question me. Your mother
Sold you at birth.
Shake hands and feel the blood
Of the other. Be quick,
Then go your ways.
It's nearly dawn.

What is Love?

Walk with me now, I'll have the setting right:
a pond, idyllic pasture, woods, an orange sun-
down, breeze, quiet.

                    Now tell me what is love. I
could conjugate hate. I could diagram cruelty.
I thrive on lust. I could write an encyclopedia
on the meaning of meanness, murder, *mal*.
I don't know what is love. What is love?

1.

La Barucci, courtesan, hit hard times:
Broke, consumption, the parties gone.
Paul Demidoff, good man, in Paris,
Paid her to sit in a good strong wind,
And he would drown her with Seltzer water.
Demidoff laughed. La Barucci coughed and was paid.
Then, soon, *la Dame aux camellias* died.
—Tell me, tell me. What is love?

2.

"Even such is Time which takes . . . in trust"
                                 our beauty.
Would I love you scarred? Would I love you
Lost in insanity? Or would I turn and go
To some exotic place where beauty is always?
Before you answer, What is love?

3.

The mother will kill for her babe.
The father will kill for his friend.
The lover will kill for his love.

Each one will walk away
At the drop of a word.
Each one will live in hate
At the drop of a word.
Tell me, What is love?

Even with this setting, you have not answered me.
The sun is down. Night sounds come from the woods
and from the pond. You have walked away.
I stand in darkness with my question.
The moon's false light comes on. Why did you
not answer—at least, that you didn't know?

Back for the Last Funeral:
The Old Rugged Cross

I remember no stations of the cross, only
An old rugged cross in the song and wanting
To get away from the church and shrieking voices.
Wanting to say to Mrs. Grover, "Blast it out
Your other end."

Wanting to leave that church, town,
That anywhere I was and head for the next
Rising or setting sun. Win my way with a grin.
I knew I was handsome. Then I was.

I knew I was not to be trusted. Cocky
And stupid, I didn't know this:
I was not to be trusted by me.

Riding the freights, I always knew the time
And place to jump. And the time and place
To climb back on. Gone are the wives.

Lives, quick tricks. I hardly remember them.
I never knew how bored I would be.
Some kind of conscience—or magnet—I didn't know
about
Brought me back to this church and grave.

My pockets full of money, I want to get out of here.

The punk who drives my car
Will take me anywhere. I don't have to tell him.
"Booze, sweetheart?" he will say. "Want me to play a tape?"

The Children

The children play in the street.
One boy always wears a red
Shirt and rides a bicycle. Some
Of the others chase him.

Few cars go by, and they
Are slower than the children.

I watch from behind sheer
Curtains that won't be quiet.
My heart won't be quiet. These
Are not children.
They never go into the houses.
When night comes they disappear.

Late afternoons, they're wildest,
And strong enough to be soldiers—
Pushing and shoving, and pulling in
The strength of the sun.
Somebody should call the police.

The Coronary

Some people think Georgia
Is Georgia the same all over. They confuse
Cotton in a cotton patch
With the pink nylon shirt they wear to the grocery store.
Those same people don't know
Mississippi is not Alabama. (Who
Could never go to Oregon and think
It was Washington?) Say *Atlanta*,
They don't even think of Georgia, and
Never of Mississippi. Florida
Is Florida—where people go. They might
Fly witless over Alabama.

Break down five minutes
In the Louisiana wilds—or a main
Street in a hamlet between Alexandria
And New Orleans: women so extraordinary,
Shopping for lace and cake mix, they
Bounce you off the road map.
                              They could.
Only: the costly car and your money expertise
Eliminate you. Royal Street
Is towards the bottom of the map—
More readily yours by plane. In Nachitoches,
Hearts don't pump. Never did. Nobody grieves.

Pretty girls don't spread their legs
For handsome boys. In the middle
Of the morning, really nothing happens,
For the sun doesn't rise.
                                    Unless, friend,
Business or compulsion to drive
Your Mercedes has pushed you
To the outskirts of a town whose name
You can't pronounce, and your heart
Begins to act without excuse, and your
Car goes wild off the road. From a window,
A native sees it and calls an ambulance.

Translating in Brazil

I.

One afternoon or morning, London and growing
Orchids may be most of you today. Tomorrow,
Money: transferals, interest rates, selling land
You knew you loved, speculating.
                                    (A baby is
A history: driven down upon by sun, forced
To dream, it cries for milk that takes it from
The ordinary blues and yellows back to dream.)

Last summer all he wanted was conjugal.
Now, he's tired of that. A naked leg recreates
A scene. But it's noon. He rushes through
Bodies he doesn't see. Then the place he meets
You for lunch: drinks, the sprawling out
Ambition for his son.
                        The woman sprawled
On her back porch late in the afternoon.
Her legs aren't shaved. "I don't care," she says
As she drinks beer from a can. "If he's in
That bitch, let him look at my hairy legs."
Mrs. Watson nods but doesn't agree. All the time,
Sun is seeping through trees, preparing a scene
For distance.
                Now we have a scene and mystery.

No voices. The woman and Mrs. Watson are there,
Pencil sketches. They have been dead for years.
The woman did shave her legs. Mrs. Watson
Moved to Detroit and lived a terrible life.

II.

The beginning of a new month, September—with its
Craziness, the ordinary vacations over, some trees
In this part of the country ready for change, less
Pink and white to look at in flowers — we are
Brothers in one body. What I swore I would do
Years ago, I have done, and I send you a picture
Postcard from Australia. I've carefully chosen the
Colors so they're like what's back home. You must
Stay with your wife. She's a receptionist, and you
Need the money. All of us need it. Who would
Havethought yesterday—you most of all—I'd
Be sleeping under a foreign quilt tonight? Who would
Have thought you'd be sitting in a lazy tavern with
A woman you don't like and whose name you don't
Know, reading my post card and showing her the picture?
Two more drinks and she's drunk, and we're together.
We're not at ease. We're like brothers who shook hands
Twenty years ago and said goodbye. One of us staying

On the farm to help father, the other going to New York.
The first plane ride. You may think we're a million
People. We're not. Nobody in Malaysia swaps wives
The way we do. Nobody in Kansas or Mississippi
Has left the farm you left and waved to his brother
From the plane the way you did. Nobody else wore
The brown tie. I still have it in the back of a closet.
I smell it sometimes to know if you are there. The color
Is faded, the tie smells old, but the label is the same,
And I think I remember how the tie cut into your neck.
The faded brown is one of the colors we celebrate,
You in the tavern, a stranger with a stranger, and
The two of us here shaking hands again for a moment.

III.

Between their talk of politics, men on corners, ask:
Who would believe she's the woman? They
Ruminate and confuse themselves with pictures on the
Sports page, pitchers they read about this morning
And All-American tackles whose Polish names they
Can't remember. You lived with them, somebody says.
They're ashamed and look at their big feet or off
At a tree where a miracle is happening. Or back to her
Where she sits, younger, at ten o'clock opening time

In the Huddle Bar. She is not older, their eyes
Could tell them, if they looked. They don't look
Beyond a world of smog and miracles they create all
Day. Her smile is more fixed. It's almost a lasting
Smile, but you would know it, if you wanted to,
From the photograph in her wallet. When dresses were long
And hair was short. She remembers them—not a gang
But each with a juke box song and particular shadows
Of an afternoon or night that made them what they are.
They're confused in other ways. They think they're each
Other. Tuesday nights, after bowling, their wives can't
Tell them apart. This is interrupted, though, by dreams,
When they're real again, and by the minutes while they
Drink coffee and wake up. If their children remember
Them it's by noise: bed springs, slamming doors,
Once when they might have wept, muttered sounds
That meant no. Hearing a new song played, she
Sees in the bar's mirror exact faces and she hears
Weeping that turns into laughter. "They forget who
I am," she tells the bartender. He holds a wineglass
To the light. "They confuse me with July and August.
I always go away those months—to Florida—to
Collect myself. I come back new, and they don't know me."

IV.

Last Thursday was different. He's more used to himself.
A calendar framed in red sits on the card table. That's
Where he lost himself in the Galapagos Islands, and
Where his eyes, as they open from sleep, tell him he
Must put on his glasses to discover what day it is.
Sheltered by dawn, he could almost do a dance.
Yesterday and last night, he heard his father speaking.
He remembers the words but not how the voice sounded.
What happened? There was wind drowning car mufflers
And babies were crying. There was a storm in the east.
Thunder rolled. What's gone is gone, but he's better.
His head is bandaged. His head begins to ache. But
He's better. The world already screaming, dawn turning
Scarlet, he smiles. He will sleep again.

                                                You might
Question all this. You might say: "I'll write a letter
Before I forget—and find out the facts." I'd speak
If I could and tell you to do it. One evening,
When everybody's gone to the movies, you will eat
An apple and watch baseball on TV. While the
Bases are loaded, you will think: "There's something
I didn't do and don't want to do ever." Nothing
Will happen much. The Giants will win the game. You'll
Win your bet. Everybody will tell you about the movie.
Nevertheless, I will wish we had written the letter.

V.

His last journey South, they didn't see each other.
Their lawns met, their houses were side by side,
But there were hedges and curtains, shades at night.
They usually slept at different hours. Once, throughout
The summer, they talked on the phone. Her voice,
A collection of air over miles of wire, came from next
Door as he knew it when he was five. After that, they
Didn't need to see each other. He writes her from St. Louis
And omits anything new. Another time, he sends a picture
From outer space. "This is a picture of us," he writes
On the back. "Use your magnifying glass. I think
You can find us." Dear woman that she is, she finds
Them: he's in a jet, flying from St. Louis to Omaha.
She's hanging out clothes. She holds a clothespin in her
Left hand. "We're rich," he writes in another letter.
"We think we know each other. The sun comes down the
same
For you every day. Your camellias bloom and I see you
Beside them at evening. We're not disappointed. I tell you
We're rich with love." In his will, he's left her
Everything. It's this that worries him. Maybe she won't
Want the painting by Chagall. The picture of a dog
Chased by a boy and running through a pasture might
Have to be stored. The Chagall might be put in

A shed with spiders, and she will worry. "What
Will I do with the money? How can I explain a new dress?"
It's then he decides to change his will, over and over.
Monday, if he's alive, he'll go to his lawyer. "Everything,"
He says, relieved, "goes to the state. Any state. Where
Your grandmother was born." Nothing uncommon
Happens to her for decades. "We're children," he writes.
"People forget we're all another person. Love as always."

VI.

It's not a hotel now. When it was, the man and wife
Met him in his room. They drank an average-priced
Bourbon that Sunday. The wife might know what they
Talked about. They all can remember the energy. Ambition
Must have rattled the door. Poor Jefferson Hotel, it had
A lobby big enough for Heaven and small enough
For you to spot your friends. The man and wife, whatever
You say about them, are still together. The man, whoever
He is, is known by name in all the cities. Except
By you, the third one in the room. Your room, but there's
No hotel. When you see his name in a newspaper, you
Have to translate, as you do Portuguese in Brazil. You
Think it should be Spanish: you set up a room with
A double bed, put bourbon and ice on a dresser top, hang

On the wall a picture nobody sees. Then you move to energy
And ambition, talk and talk. People's names are
Mentioned. Are they still worth mentioning? I have
A snapshot of the three of you. I compare it with pictures
I see of him in the papers. His hair is longer now, fitting
The fashion. There are changes enough to number the days
But I can't see them. His wife and I look the same.
My eyes are different today, more intense, for I wear
Glasses. Soon we'll meet—all three—and I'll pretend
I know you. I'll tell myself we're still in that room. We're
Pouring bourbon over ice that hasn't melted. We're laughing.

In this room, I see an elephant coming towards me. He's
Somewhere in Africa. He's determined, I can tell. His ears
Flare like flowers. He won't harm me. He'll go through me
And the wall and come back again from the other wall.
Without fear, I look down. I light a cigarette. I study
My fingernails and the ring on my finger. Easily, I
Accept the elephant. I welcome him. Sometimes, when
I go astray, I wonder why he's alone.

VII.
A baby. A baby is a fugue. Nothing but Time
Is rigid. It moves to the rhythm it creates. That is its
Form. Your passion for orderly days, for pink camellias
Blooming again when the calendar tells you they should—
This is deception and nonsense. Which we breathe.

from

Flight
(1981)

"In a sense, on my self alone rests the common dignity which I cannot allow to be
debased either in myself or others."
—Albert Camus, *L'Homme révolté*

(*1862. A young man from Winston County, Alabama, is searching for Union
troops in order to join them. Through the forest he must try to protect himself
from both Unionists and Confederates.*)

Remembering

One September afternoon, before we
Married, I said to Martha, "We are
Alone." We sat by the spring where
Mama kept her milk and butter cool.
"What do you mean?" She put her hand
On mine. I remember her hand was scratched
From berry-picking. What did I mean?
—For birds were singing everywhere.
Just over the hill, you could hear
Tom Caleb yelling at his wife and boys.
"I'll be gone," I said, "one of these
Days, away from these hills, and if
I come back, I won't come back
To a blessed thing but you."

A Source

After I had sat that day, all day,
That 4th of July, and heard Chris Sheats
And the other men talk about our Union,
I rode my mare Old Belle the 15 miles
To home and Martha. I lay beside my wife
And told her what all happened:
'It was too hot to get your breath. Over
Two thousand people. Babies bawling.
Some fights broke out. But we decided
Not to go with the State. To go our own
Way and let the others do what they want.
And Uncle Dick Payne—he's against us—
Yelled, "The Free State of Winston!"'

Martha went to sleep, but I was
Hot, there wasn't a breeze, and I kept
Thinking: Free. How free? From what?
Ourselves. Ourselves? Nonsense.

Letter to Martha

Martha—Love—I don't know where
I am—I know I'm in these woods—
And where East is and North—I
Know which way you are—I just
Don't know when to go—how far—
I don't know where—and if I
Get to where it is—if that is right—
I think I know where not to stay —
I want to be with you— want to touch
Your face—I hope this gets to you—
I'll let you hear—Don't let them
Get you down—I love you—Jim

Hiding

All answers to any questions are the woods and night:
Insects, animals rustling. For all
I know, right here is the Globe. But if
I knew I have a wife called Martha, and Martha
Has our child inside her, would I want that to be?
Pain in my leg, pain in my heart:
Would I say now to the child-boy-man,
'Be severed from much you love, rebel with reason
And love (or what you think they are)'?
Would I say this and break for you the charm
We think of as happiness? I know one answer:
Whatever I said, I would be a murderer.

Word From Home

They will win, I know. We will
Win. Old Glory will win. But I
Have lost everything. My wife has
Died in childbirth. They shot Papa,
And Mama died because she wanted to.
I look up at these stars tonight,
And I try to talk to a God I try
To understand. I would like to know
Some things before I die. All I know
Is I have a broken leg and I
Am hungry and sad and I
Didn't do the things they told me to.

An Ending

Who is my enemy? Am I my
Enemy? When I move, I make sound.
When I breathe, I call my killers.
Why is the wind so loud in the leaves?
I see my father dead.
I see his face through the trees,
On the moon.
Have I killed myself?
Would no blood drop
If a knife cut through my chest?
I am afraid.
I think I was never born.
I think my father is the moon.
I think my cousins are the wind.

from

My Confidant, Catullus

(1983)

I.
Advice from Catullus

My friend Catullus, always aware
Of everything high and mighty and low
And discordant, tells me to beware of
People who speak or dress too nicely, and
People who do the opposite. "Caesar,
At his best, is comfortable and wise."

I listen to Catullus and believe him.
Then suddenly dressed like a peacock,
Perfumed, off on another passionate journey
To Clodia's. His last words to me
As he prepares a speech: "Will I out-do
Her brother? How is the sound of my voice today?"

Catullus Reads My Manifesto

Put off by fashion—Manhattan
To Indian reservations—I handed
Catullus my manifesto.
"It's all right." He gave it back.
All dressed up at 10 AM,
He mixed me a screwdriver.
I lit a cigarette, pushed back
My hair, preparing myself.
"I don't see a hill—green, brown,
Blue—or a tree, much less a flower
Screaming its yellow heart
At the sun. Write as you please,
Only—and don't take offense—
Write me beautiful women, particular
Ones, or ugly women, particular
Ones, or in-between, particular
Ones, to read about. Or
The river, yellow as a lemon peel,
You didn't mention."
                    "I might
As well get drunk," I said.
He mixed me another screwdriver.

You Asked Me

You really want my opinion,
Catullus? I wouldn't touch her.
You'll probably get syph, front and back.
That young man she's been sleeping with—
He takes anything to bed: man, woman, dog.
Marijuana and a little booze, he's ready.
I know you don't want my opinion.
But I'd wash her up and check her out
And see if that boy's in the closet.

Who is the Real Catullus?

Gaius Valerius Catullus, listen
To this: you're like Keats, Wordsworth,
Dylan Thomas, Scott Fitzgerald, Thomas Wolfe,
Alexander the Great, and Custer. Yes,
I said Custer. This critic or scholar—
Whatever—said it here in this book.

Give me a show. I'd like a Custer-
Wordsworth-Dylan Thomas act.
No, a Thomas Wolfe-Alexander the Great.
Dammit, I can't decide.
They all sound good.

Who were you last night
In Clodia's bed? Did you tell her
To wait for the real Catullus?

Don't throw that book at me.

Catullus Sends a Dinner Invitation

If I had your gall, Catullus,
I wouldn't worry about the phone bill
Or the end of the month
Or how much you owe for last year's
Income tax. You could live
On ink and my sweat. I saw
The dinner invitation you sent:
Bring your own food (and make sure
I'll like it), a beautiful woman,
And a good wine. Don't forget
Witty talk, and you have to do
The laughing.
                    I know. You don't
Have to tell me. He might even show
And you could get drunk and flirt
With the woman. If he doesn't,
You'd be depressed anyway.

Alas, But Not Too Literally

Catullus,
I have no Caesar
To declaim. Look at us:
Never at war
Yet fighting
War after war.
Nothing, not a thing
I write will be read
By any Head
Of State.
I might say, "I berate
You heartily, Senator
And President."
But I wouldn't be sent
For, reprimanded, or
Cajoled, or commanded
To ease up. Instead,
As I told you, I wouldn't be read.
I'm deader than Clodia's sparrow, Catullus.

To Lesbia's Sparrow

Fly, sparrow, back to the breast
Of Lesbia. You have worried me
Long enough at my window. She
Has grieved, she says. Better, go
To Catullus: he has made such a
Fool of himself, wanting to touch
The bird that touched Lesbia's breast.
Go anywhere. I'm sick of you.
You've made a fool of everybody.

Late Night Talk With Catullus

It is late, and after much wine
We are familiar.
          "Catullus," I ask,
"Does it bother you what they say
about your Clodia: that she sleeps
with her brother, that she goes out disguised
at night and picks up whatever tramp
is walking the streets of Rome?"

"I love her."

"Which means—?"

"I love her."

"It's more than lust?"

"Much more, because it's hopeless."

II.
Catullus Mad Song:

He is a gallows bird
If ever I saw one:
His pockets full of the country's silver,
His face always contorting
(One face for Clodia, one for his wife,
One for the boy, another for Caesar,
And on, endlessly).
He has no face.

Once he was caught
With the silver in his hands,
Caught on the back of a boy
With Clodia watching.
His wife, in another part
Of the house, told reporters,
"Appearances are deceptive."

And then he wrote a book
About it all. Somehow,
Instead of the clap, he got religion.
And richer. Where could I damn him

To, that's not worn out or full?
Caesar doesn't read his book. Clodia

Doesn't read. His wife had a perfectly
Planned collapse.

Who reads my epigrams?
A couple of people who once were friends.

Uncollected Poems

Drawing Beasts

No matter how I try,
when I draw beasts
they are not scary.
They are either funny or sad or
full of longing for a proper landscape
or somebody you'd like to have
to your house for cocktails
on a stormy afternoon.
I have looked around
in my nightmares,
but I find no scary beasts.
With a man, it's different.
I can draw a man who's
so afraid, he scares me
half to death. My beast with
three heads makes me want to ask,
"Would all of you like a martini?"

The Daily Caller

Every day he knocks at the
Door, and every day I tell him,
Through the wood, that I'm not
Here. From the pantry window,
I watch him get in a black Cadillac
And drive away. He's in his twenties,
Blond, and dressed stylishly. He's
Almost like an *Esquire* ad.

Sometimes he leaves notes—a child's
Handwriting—which make no sense:
You should come out and see the sun.
You'll forget how to talk. There's
A sale at Wilson's Men's Shop. Spring
Weather is almost here. What do you
Look like? Somebody wants to meet you.

He's not to be trusted. I think he sells
Insurance, or magazines. Or maybe he's
An extortionist. I'll figure him out, but—
Meantime—what good could a young man do
Who knocks at your door and drives a Cadillac?
This was his note today: *They're killing all*
The whales. Three people died last night
At Memorial Hospital—where were you?
You think you want to be alone but you don't.

The Cosmological Man

In the carefully unlit place
Where you are having what you hoped
Was a very dry drink,
The man beside you is on the brink
Of madness. He is political,
He is sociological.
The piano breaks its back
For a sotto voce "As Time Goes By."
Who will have the heart attack
First, you or the cosmological man?
He's gone finite now:
His wife, his mistress, his life in bed.
You start to leave but instead
Lean to him and—sotto voce—say,
"Comfort me with silence
For I am sick of your love."
His silence is brief, and now
He's straddling the universe.

On Reading Roethke's Letters

Poets are as trivial and mean
as anybody, and as good
at gossip as any philanderer
in a bar, as phony
as most politicians. But they
profess more precisely,
and don't make money at it.
Naïve, I believe their poems.
I turn away when, in the flesh,
I'm caught between those
sons-of-bitches' egos and destruction
who ride on poets' backs.

Gertrude Stein: II

She lashed with a pious
    Redundant tongue;
The world an audience at tea.

Some said:
    The clothes too fine
    For these old things
        Of mine.

Some said:
    Heretic, discolored by
    Barbaric dye.

And some
    Were young
    And took a dozen cups
    Of tea

And bared their backs.

And later showed
Profound and lovely scars.

Catullus Mad Song III

Tell Caesar to hump another young boy
And leave me alone.
No, tell him to visit Nixon at San Clemente.
They should have much to talk about.
And tell him I don't take back
What I wrote in the epigram he saw.
Say I have him humping a goat
In the epigram I'm writing now,
And the goat is Rome,
And tell him the odor is awful.

Weather

I.

The extremity of the hour
Demands it. The old woman
With the rose over her ear
Is deaf. She is blind. She holds
A goose and asks it where to go.
Her voice is a whistle. The goose,
If it knows, cannot understand.
And so she clings to what
She can feel: the goose, rain,
The sun going down. The extremity
Of each hour demands the rose,
Brought to her fresh by a child.

II.

I am like the weather
On a building. I am the fool.
My nose has struck itself
On the bottom of a brook. I say:
Minnows beware. Come closer.
My blood goes out in smoke.
—Now, on an ugly Easter
Morning, I must trace myself.
This is impossible.
—Now, in this wind, I'm through.

VIII.
Time is arithmetic. The wonderful
Corpse studies it in an almanac.
His other wife is calling: *The clouds
Are so dark it looks like rain. Come in!*
He cannot hear. He has wept longer
Than any Jew. Alone—forever—
He would lose his eyes.

IV.
Weather is lightning and ice, it indulges
Seasons. There are nights when martyrs beg
For a candle. Weather catches a landscape
In a frame: outrules the rulers, the cow
And the goose, the old woman holding the goose
And led by a cow. I am lost in a snow storm.
I float on red water. What good are signs
And arithmetic? The one who understands is a witch
With a rose over her ear.

Seattle

If you're living, dark lady,
And not too old to read,
I'm the Army kid you picked up,
Just before closing time,
At the Hi-Lo Bar.

It was love at first sight,
But it didn't last long on my pay;
Two nights and a day and
You'd had me. Or I'd had you.

If you're dead or in an old
Folks' home for hookers—wherever —
I wish you well. It was important,
And I hope you weren't too bored.

To Miss X

If you're alive, so many of you,
But you, especially,
Who used to, years ago
When I was a child,
Slam out of the Methodist Church
At Sunday noon if the preacher
Went over the hour one minute,
I address you.

And who dyed your hair
Black as could be.
And who had your trysts
Over chocolate sodas
At the Haleyville Drug Store.
Yes, with married men,
While the powdered ladies
Whispered. I love you.

Near Point Mallard, Decatur, Alabama

Green: the hundred-year-old
Trees, baggy oaks, and green
Hanging in baskets from the limbs—
Even the trunks are green, moss and ivy,
And merge with garden and lawn and pasture.

The mind lifts to hills.
                    There is a single
Green, not bothered by, out of the eye's
Corner, the red barn and the white silo.

In a ditch, a rust-red gash
Hidden by kudzu, Genesis—Genesis Jesus—
Washes down sardines and crackers
With Kentucky bourbon.
. . . and a married woman
is a big attraction
even when I
cain't git my
satisfaction. . .
He taps his foot to his singing.
Green snakes and rattlers scurry.

And, tell me, who doesn't want
His boy to be something special,

Something a daddy can talk about?
And so, being poor and needing teeth
And food for the teeth, he needed a savior,
And so he named his son that way.

Your hand lighting a cigarette
Disturbs the green—the dogwood,
The camellia bush—and to the cadence
Of a breeze, green turns silver.

You see him,
                    somebody, something—
White shirt, dark pants—
Rise out of the green like a god.
You see a miracle move slowly across
The pasture,
Slowly towards the gravel road
Out of your sight,
And you know, as your eyes follow,
You must allow a miracle to happen.
Must in a way, sponsor it.

The miracle,
                    But you don't know

What it is—a god—though you have set
Its place of habitation:

                          Genesis Jesus drunk
And lighting out for a woman.

                               In town
Or on a country dust road, you
Have seen him or a cousin or one
Of his bastard children.

                          You have seen
His father, now dead, who never
Got his teeth; gummed it to the grave.
He damned his son to hell.

                             But,

Even son, miracle,

                    your miracle:
Your creation out of time and colored space,
Your merman out of a green sea.

Only the dark pants,
Blue and dirty, foreshadow
Your mauve evening and what will be
Night, dark as a coal mine,
The coal mine he left for you to enter.

The fig tree is black, and
Beyond, your memory of hills climbing
Green into sky, and beyond, morning and night.

But, tell me this, who
Wouldn't—a daddy, I mean—
Send the no-count bastard to hell,
Raise up his gun and tell him?

What I Meant

I.

Where is the fire?
The trees are not on fire.
All the windows in this house
Tell me.

I am used to silence,
Its sound,
From inside trees
And the hearts of stones.
I am used to the noise
Of where I was
In photographs.

The siren raping the night:
An ambulance for my heart attack?
Already.
I know I said, "Come quietly."

II.

Last night was my last
Night here.
I was up late packing:
Six Bibles, my notebook, sea shells,
My memory of a guitar I couldn't play

And of a man playing a guitar and
Singing and walking to the highway,
Photographs with heads scraped off.

I said over and over,
"What will the pine trees do
Without me?"
Leaving,
I hardly noticed the pines.

When the taxi came, it was raining.
I said goodbye
When I said good morning
To the driver.

III.
Years ago—1947—I wrote down:
"When it says *No Tresspassing*,
Stop." I always want to go on.
I want to look back where I've been
And say, "That's where I was.
This is what I meant."
The fool I am, I haven't learned
My basics. I have to review
All the time. It's not wilderness
I want: it's going on too far.
Where I've been.

IV.
Now I'm here—somewhere—in this place
Of camellias. They are named Perfection.
My blood says these are funeral flowers,
A blanket of pink camouflage.
Camellias bloom in January. They bloom
And die.
Then gardenias. The air is white and sweet.
I'm dazed. I want to hide.

V.
I took my last journey today.
It is the pavement outside
That leads to a gravel road
And then paths. So much of where
I go is private property.

Crooked Creek and Shady Grove Church
And Harmony School
Linger in wilderness.
Lizards are quick as blinking eyes.
Snakes dream in the sun
And I caress them.

For My Son

Like a wizard of true magic
I devise for you
Openings, unseen, to escape
The burning car, the lying
Friends, the screaming wife,
The bottle of sleeping
Pills. And you move
From hero to hero: passing
The football, touching the woman's
Breast, signing the contract,
Drinking the fifth martini.
Your eyes are human enough
To cry but only with joy
At beauty. You can't lie;
There's nothing to lie about.
Time takes no toll: your
Beauty is dignity, your laughter
Is wisdom. Even when death
Is far off, you walk towards
God.

   Towards God, who will,
I trust, keep these words
From your eyes.

The Goldfish Pond, Under the Oaks, in August

—suggested by one of Nabokov's lectures

In the deep of the country, in Alabama, what do these orange fish,
Sheathed by warm water, dream about? Winter,
With the pond's top frozen, or fall,
With leaves as orange as they, obliterating
Their sky?
           Past hummingbirds, you follow them
To the eye, the mind, the soul—mixed with orange,
Movement, shade, diamonds of light.
And then you imitate, proceed, go beyond
Recklessly, as the fish discover the oaks, the oaks
Imagine your dead friend, still young,
Walking in from the rain, closing his umbrella,
And saying: "Let's stroll through the fern garden
And look at the goldfish." And you do, and dream
With the fish till they are you and your friend,
Gold beneath ice and under orange leaves.

Things

The lover scanning his mistress's scribble or her scowling brows is learning to read. So is the theologian comparing the ideas of eros and agape. . . —I.A. Richards

In this silence my pen and I are unworthy
To talk:
  the sun comes up and shatters together
My book of Corman's translation of Ponge's *Things,*
The pad of paper emerging white, the cigarette
Ash emerging gray . . .

Yesterday, a punch-drunk boxer,
Drunk, opening up the pool hall
With me. "Where is the Greyhound
Station?" he'd just come from,
And I said, "Down the street, take
A left." And he said, "Are you kidding?
I got a left that you ain't seen." And
He shadow-boxed my face. Sun
Through the window glorified the scar
On his chin. "And money," he said,
"I still ain't broke," as he took
Five dollars out of his shoe.
Please listen.
Have I turned out to be my uncles:

A preacher without a religion; old
Before I'm old; spitefully young
When I should be reclining on a lawn
Chair and dreaming of orchards;
A bed-hopper with bastards all over
The kudzu-covered country; a drunk
Without recourse?

Vague through heat waves and my failing
Glasses, the man up the street has a walk
Not mastered, a walk without grace
(And I think of my friend's walk, effortless
But in command of a street or a room).

                      I can see
The pants are royal blue and the bleached white
Shirt is a glare in the sun of 29 August;
And I think, as I open the door to the restaurant
And lose the man forever, there might be a sign
Of overwhelming sagacity in his brown
Or blue or gray or no-color eyes.

Could it be I've turned what's lovely—
The profound, the brutal, the scarred, the gentle:
The innocent—into things?

My father, old and wise and therefore lost,
Stands in the crazy barn of a store
In the shopping-center hell,
Stands at the chrome stile where no one may enter.
His face, too brown from too much sun,
Is innocent, bewildered, accepting,
Is kind to us who are the ones responsible.
And says (nothing spoken),
Tom, you understand all this.
And I answer (nothing spoken),
I don't.
I shove, I curse (nothing outward,
Nothing spoken
So he can't see or hear).

Alas (That Old-Fashioned Word...

On the phone he cried and said,
"Please come. She's left me."
And we did, my wife and I did,
And found him lying across the bed,
Drunk, and cursing, and saying,
"She said she won't cook me another bite."

Elegiac and sad as early mornings,
Four o'clock, with a lamp on
In one room, and from outside,
All the apartment windows dark
But one:
              That's what his face says
As he walks to the all-night diner
For coffee.

Alas
(That old-fashioned word
Popular in easy crossword puzzles),
How the mind bends.

When I was a boy, I took my
Summers in Nashville: the properly
Settled and rich part of the family
Had hills for a background, horses,

Trees and shrubs whose names I didn't
Know. Guided by the Southern manner,
I wore what I should—what was stylish
And, more important, what was proper—
To promenade down Church Street and have
A soda in the then-elegant Candyland
Where everyone knew my cousins.
Short pants and a matching jacket.
I like to think the afternoons were fun
And the purple evenings, blinking
With lightning bugs, serene.
I like to think the Palm Beach pants
Didn't itch, that the wide picture of morning
To night was almost static beauty.

       But the tableau
Is a lie, for everything moved,
Was moving then, has moved, and
The costumes changed.

      What remains
Of me is pathetic: outward manners
Nobody understands, and eyes that refuse to see.

School Being Over

Cambodia mirrors
Yesterday and tomorrow,
My greed and yours.
New kinds of death—less merciful—
Sniff at the door.

Does
It justify to say:
The poem is less ambiguous
Than the formula, more
Merciful than instamatic dying?
(Poet of Greece Simonides
Left these words among the atoms:
Traveler, tell the men of Sparta:
We who lie buried here
Did what they told us to.
—Or have we a question?)

There is no Solomon's ring for anyone
Except the truly mad man,
And so the question's question . . .

Are we the figures on the movie screen?
Are we what we watch on television?
I had a vision:

                    The news
            At five o'clock and six
            Is a lie; the blood is the heart
            Of a makeup man; the bombs
            Are MGM; the screaming,
            Twentieth Century; the children Paramount.
            All, United Artists.

in the Algonquin Bar
ladies must be escorted.
Babe: Auden said "...the occupational disease
            Of poets is frivolity."
Allen: And I agree. Another martini?
Babe: Yes, please. And if you read Kierkegaard,
            Who's probably dead like God...
Allen: Next you'll send me to Aristotle.
            And, furthermore, they all play games
            With words. Not even the OED
            Can explain the shifts and shadings.
Babe: Darling, we have to have something for —
            To start from. We're not born free.
Allen: Can't we look at what's there,
            And do what we can, and try to learn?
Babe: You're hopeless.

Allen: No. You like to talk.

Babe: It's why I'm here. My way of action.

Allen: Your beat is fashion. The comings and goings.
Auden also said, or wrote,
In a moment of lucidity or doubt or both
Something like this: *the existentialist's choice,*
Pascal's wager, Kierkegaard's leap
Are all fine for "dramatic literature,"
But are they true?"
                    I have
A feeling that Hegel sometimes thought,
"Oh, what a bright boy am I."

Babe: Next time we talk, we won't have martinis.

Allen: I don't think we'll talk again.

St. Jude:
Even after the swagger, and you know it was swagger,
And you've learned what the diamond and ruby are,
And it's come to you one afternoon that your life
Is one more soap opera or grade B movie,
And you have turned to Alcohol or LSD or Speed
(Not as the young do, but after Knowledge),
and you sit alone in New Orleans at a bar on Royal,
and no one sees you and you don't see—

I tell you there is hope.

I am simple. Don't turn away because of that.

You are not before a camera. You are not a camera.

Walk down Royal, turn to Bourbon.

Look and see but do not record.

TV: *"One life to live and regret."*
Living Color.

Dr.: But what if the baby wants to live?

Angela: It hasn't a chance with a father like Allen.

Dr.: But who has a chance? And Allen is all I hear.

    I'll be the baby's father.

    I love you Angela.

Angela: I want to abort. It's the only thing.

    I wasn't born for the likes of this.

Dr.: Of what? We could go away. Live happily ever after.

Angela: After what? Besides, there's no place to go.

    But beyond the moon. I want to abort.

AN IMPORTANT MESSAGE: ARE YOU REGULAR?

Coda

School being over, and death as always

    A canticle (even the final breathing),
    The frivolous poet must, by his nature, love.

Does it matter much to wonder: Does it matter?
(A cameraman on the periphery might ask:

Will the ambitious mad men run for cover?
Then take electric shock to answer:
What, if anything, is missing?
—The mad are incredibly shrewd.)

Vanity rules out love. Go tell the Preacher.
Ambition rules out love. Tell the Politician.
And the Teacher. Self-love is suicide.

One gets tired of questions.
But the more they lift, mist in the valley,
Affirms, one hopes, a clearing in a further question.

Must one give up his credentials
If he's come to think
Love's not crucial for everyone?

A Stylish Adieu

That's what one of the newspapers said.
He bought champagne for every high-class hooker,
Politician, policeman, sports reporter, etc.,
In and out of sight of the steel mill town where
He was richer than anybody.

"Baseball is not just a sport, it's life."
That's when the lights went off in the big
Banquet room. All the power in that part
Of town went off. The band played
By heart "God Bless America," and we all sang
As fiercely as we could, giving courage
To the less fortunate people
Getting mugged on the dark streets.

At midnight the lights came on, in time
For the sleepy mother to say, "You've said it all."
Not a dry eye in the place.
For a long time I didn't dread strangers
In bars or taxi drivers or insurance salesmen
Or barbers or writing my friend in Patagonia.

Thomas McAfee was professor of English at the University of Missouri-Columbia before his death in 1982. He was educated at the University of Missouri-Columbia and the Kenyon School of English. His work appeared in *Esquire, Epoch, Prairie Schooner,* and elsewhere, including numerous anthologies. He was the author of ten books, including *The Body and the Body's Guest, Rover Youngblood: a Novel, I'll Be Home Late Tonight,* and *Whatever Isn't Glory.* He received a writing fellowship from the National Endowment for the Arts in 1976.

This book is set in Adobe Garamond, Sinhala, and Sweet Home Oklahoma. In 1975, BkMk Press published its first full-length poetry title by a single poet, *The Body and the Body's Guest* by Thomas McAfee. *There Is Not Fashion to It* marks BkMk's fortieth anniversary of publishing full-length poetry collections.